from the ashes

from the ashes

poems by

wayne a. gilbert

Liquid Light Press

Premium Chapbook First Edition

ISBN-10: 0983606366

ISBN-13: 978-0-9836063-6-9

Liquid Light Press

poetry that speaks to the heart

www.liquidlightpress.com

Cover Art & Design by M. D. Friedman
Back Cover Photo by Lee Rasizer

from the ashes

Preface

I had barely arrived for a retreat on the Isle of Iona in the
Hebrides off the western coast of Scotland, and moved into my cell
in the restored 1500 year-old abbey there, when my wife called with
the news that my mother had had an accident and was dying. Iona is
about as isolated as one can be in the modern world. My journey
home involved a van, two ferries, a bus, a train, a taxi and three
airplanes. The journey was complicated by an ash cloud from an
erupting Icelandic volcano that interfered with air traffic over
Europe. I did not make it home before my mother died.

These poems were written in the year following her death.
Although I am professionally educated for the Christian ministry, I
long ago gave up formal religion of any kind. This always troubled
my mother deeply, although she was reassured by my improvised,
non-traditional spiritual studies and practices. These poems came
from those studies and that practice.

These poems are dedicated to the memory of my mother, Alice
May Kirby Gilbert, and to my father, Ernest Galen Gilbert, her
husband of 61 years, whose capacities for grief and for life have
sustained and inspired me.

These poems are also dedicated to those who have lost their
mothers and cannot quite get over it—ever.

magdalena blues for my mom

(alice may gilbert, 1929-2010;
"you have set your glory above the heavens. . ." 'Psalm 8:1b)

i was born in the middle of the middle halfway fully formed
                unself-consciously unaware

my mother had already eaten her own dreams
doctors would take her blood the rest of her life

there we were   pharmaceutically altered
getting ready for childhood church television popcorn

50 years of morning devotions before the brutal desert promise
            hanged itself in the sky

i'm standing in a vacant lot between two lives

i have a small brown paper bag with a peanut-butter-and-jelly
            sandwich a bag of chips a peeled quartered apple my name
            a letter for the bus driver who never arrives

her soprano voice lands her a small part in a musical comedy solos in
            every christmas pageant a place in her father's house

when she calls me to come in for supper I do not *ever* immediately
            obey but wait to hear the 2nd verse

even when she's mad at me her magdalena voice is milk
her tone is pristine the night before her last coma

our lives are sprinkled with comas brain damage
then little birthday candles to blow out once again

we are always squeezed by darkness crowding onto our small
elevators

my mother was crazy with love spilled from her the way little girls
used to have tea parties

she was the first to use valium

i watched them convulse her week after week a wad of adhesive
tape around a stick jammed into her mouth electrodes
clamped to her temples the crack of voltage slammed into
her unrelenting memory while she ironed dad's uniform
shirts my costumes for the school play my sister's little
dresses her closet full of smart unfashionable weeping

i'm waking now an old man in the mirror grimaces after a night of
progressive degeneration
i was 13 when my first wet dreams dried in stiff patches disgusted
her
i wept for my pleasures

neither of us could change her father's height the size of his hands
the heavy weight of his bible

i stopped listening to god

she never ceased praying to that monster

once we were sitting together on the patio decades after my birth
   she suddenly slapped me I snapped out of it we finished
   our coffees our cookies

she wrote me a check for $5,000 i paid off my therapist

my mother is free of pain worry of laundry detergent
i wish she could have been the grandmother i needed her to be for
   my children parented better than i
she's free of me too

i'll be driving awhile longer i suppose between minor strokes heat
   waves cold snaps nervous breakdowns night sweats easter
   lilies tilting toward the ground
then i won't see the light change the railroad crossing the hairpin
   turn

my darkness will go out

like hers

mourning-jazz for my mom

("what are human beings that you are mindful of them. . ."
Psalm 8:4a)

when we were re-united the last time
my mother was young her head full of mirthful hair

i hear her laughing now behind the door
on my side it's raining
the cold wind has followed me home
the price of my usual luggage was too high to carry on

the ice has split herself open
my head is full of icelandic ash clouds

i'm waiting
to be
magma-borne gaseous plumes
envelopes of post-eruptive matter
job's god screaming at the inert world his new word order
solar fistulas flying out of the universe
older than the first droplets of sacred water
imprisoned miles inside arctic ice

mother says
the dark for her is sweet now lazy now as chocolate streams in thick
          milk shakes
she says her body is   light

i've walked here without a cane

waiting   waiting i'm
        medicinal herbs in a swallowed capsule
        the chemical in the head of a match to be scratched
        her last exhalation spilled into my brother's cupped hands

i press my palms against the cold wood
mirth bleeds through the heavy slab into my withered hands
runic syllables bubble up gurgle scat on my tongue

the wind offers a reedy chord
the rain picks up the rhythm

we stand on the dark porch-stage
making   m u s i c   all night long

iona mother

i was looking everywhere
i couldn't find her
not even in mortuaries crematoria graveyards
not in morgues hospitals nursing homes
not in apartment buildings retirement communities
not the gardens where elderly like to linger

i looked in distant countries too especially where they revere elders
any place an old woman might have wandered off among strangers
any place she might have accidentally fallen
under bridges alongside roadways among historic ruins

i thought she might have decided to visit her childhood places
but all those homes shops churches are long closed abandoned
scraped entirely away burned down paved over decades ago
i couldn't find her

i was just about to sit down give up when
a voice like hers laughed the way a mother laughs
when her child can't find the very last hidden egg
easter morning she said *oh keep looking child*
you'll find me keep looking child i'm in plain sight
keep looking child we'll hold each other once again

i'm still looking

dive: an out of body experience

i am swimming far far from any shore
the surface is silvery blue
scarves of jade-colored silk
dance light holding me

a mothery voice calls dive dive my darling dive
i know i'm prepared
for this i swam out here for this

she insists then pleads commands prays
i recognize that progression i'm a dad
when you cannot make for your child
the decision she must   not making is unthinkable
even the danger does not overrule the need to shout   go!

it is not a sink-or-swim moment
swimming is not allowed here except to return forever shoreward

this is a take-a-deep-breath-and-dive moment
          go against millennia of training
          reverse the natural order
          kick-my-feet-over-my-head-go-down moment

of course i'll die (whatever that means)
maybe my lungs will turn into oxygen tanks
some sub-oceanic surgeon will appear slit
gills in my thick neck maybe i'll just go
as far as i can this time head back
to the surface break through   the shiny veneer

i will have to go back again later again later again until
i find the first word broke the silence
poured out first waters before we needed dreams
to remember

dive my darling dive   dive

no exegesis please: a poet's reflection on psalm 9

*("you are the one who lifts me up from the gates of death"
Psalm 9:13b)*

1.

the psalmist talks about god in 3rd person then addresses "him"
directly often alternating
    lines as if he's processing something taking it in claiming it
then in the next nearly parallel line the poet *does* it acts it right out—

why does he tell the "lord" what the "lord" has done as if the "lord"
        didn't already know
why does he tell where the "almighty" sits as if "he" hadn't already
        spent eons sitting on that
very piece of cosmic furniture
where does the poet get the nerve to finally command god to "rise
        up" do anything at all but
lounge on "his" glorious throne

this psalmist is in a very tough spot desperate "afflicted" between his
rock and a hard
        place (so he believes don't we all)—unjustly! (so he
believes don't we all)
the poet's suffering is greater than his capacity to survive it (so he
        believes don't we all)
he is convinced he'll be crushed obliterated (so he believes don't we
all) his foes are too
        strong (so he believes don't we all) his annihilation is sure
(so he believes don't we all)

the "lord" is all the things the poet was not is not cannot become
the "lord" is a ruthless merciless warrior ally (so he believes don't we
all) who destroys
                enemies hacks them to pieces even after they've fallen
                        bowed down "rebukes"
                each "blots" them out every one perishes (so he believes
                        don't we all)
the "lord" finally rights all wrongs rules absolutely "judges" from
                "his" impenetrable fortress the entire world all in "ruins"

the poet's ancestors their sacred writings have told him
it has always been so (so he believes don't we all)
it will always be so (he believes)
"rejoice in your deliverance" they tell him to declare

2.
then in the middle of his poem we meet the poet himself
he lives between two perfect times where the first noble truth reigns
"see what we suffer" he pleads "be gracious to me"
the poet lives where the wicked still win where violence hatred
                greed prevail again again again the reader can feel his pain

the poet watches his people cramped in poverty refugee slums
                outside the city blistered battered beaten into the blood-
                urine- shit-soaked earth marched in droves through "the
                gates of death" do not return

the poet walks among the trampled remnant must console each cry
        for them all lift up   their pain sing the "lord's" praises raise
        up shout out the universal chant of helpless hopeless
        oppressed people everywhere every age
"rise up o lord!" "rise up o lord!" "rise up o lord!"

the poet must always speak honestly make his voice as true as a
        tuned string go deeper into the hearts of his people than
        they have ever gone
most importantly the poet must inspire god to act :
            there's people living in misery out there
            beyond your "stronghold"
            come on get out here   give us a hand
              how about a little help for the weary
              a little less help for the wicked
then psalm 10 opens
        "why o lord do you stand far off ?
        why do you hide yourself in times of trouble?"
even his editors could see how serious the psalmist was about his
        voice

3.
i always wanted to be this poet believe in his righteous god
alas i do not belong to his tribe though i know many of their stories

my poetry comes now from a cave far from the post-war wars having
        walked the ravaged streets of those ruined cities where
        suffering stinks to high heaven cable network   preachers
        shill for their propped-up gods

i sit here cross-legged holding my grief in one hand my joy in the
            other with nothing to say about god   except
                                                i miss "him"
            the way a son grieves for his just-deceased mother
            his heart aches for his poor father who will have to
                        find ways to live without her after 60 years
            for his brother sister who cannot help wanting her
                        back for just a little while longer
            for the solace of strong loving arms now ashes
                        interred beneath a pretty
                        white cross

my psalmist friend would understand that he would
come sit awhile with me
we would
wonder weep together
                        "for the needy will not be forgotten
                        nor the hope of the poor perish forever"

take heart

("how long will you hide your face from me?" Psalm 13:1b
"in the night also my heart instructs me" Psalm 16:7b)

i say   my heart aches   i am heart-broken

i say   i have a heavy heart   my heart hurts

yearns

i'm not reporting cardiac arrest cardio-vascular disease congestive
         heart failure

my heart has nothing to do with aortic integrity ventricular function
         average blood pressure adequate pulse nothing to do with
         delivering oxygen vital nutrients to distant body parts
         carrying waste away

my heart is always about meta-physical balance
         monitoring my undetectable role in the universe
         adjusting my cosmic attitude
         syncing this speck of dust with the original bang-flow
         tuning this tiny note to the first exploding sun-chord

my heart knows itself better than i
it is my universal translator my inner gyroscope my stalwart sextant
my heart always knows the way   especially when i don't
without it i am lost a space-walker whose cord is severed whose ship
         has drifted away

when i say my heart is broken i'm saying some catastrophic force has
         crushed the link between my heart and me

the scope of the catastrophe determines how crushed how
            irreparable the link will be how long the link will be
            unreliable unavailable down how long deeply i will grieve
            when i will smile again about the future when i might feel
            like doing the least little thing stop being so disoriented
            tired i need to lie down

i'm saying before my mother died she was in a coma entirely cut off
            from us from herself from her god until she finally exhaled
            one last time without attempting to inhale ever again

i'm saying after practicing 30 years my life's work has been taken
            from me now i don't know what to do

i'm saying the body my mom's body labored into this world the body
            i've used for two-thirds a century has serious circuitry
            malfunctions they're irreversible progressive of
            course that's life "so it goes" mister vonnegut opined
i'm saying my body is cut off from my body it can't talk to me to itself

when my heart aches the pain drags me under i can only imagine
            drowning in it forever   this pain here-and-now this pain
            will always persist
i am this weight this me who cannot shake it deny it cannot resist
            its own heaviness dragging us down

when my heart yearns it is both heart and me longing for each other
one leaning toward   the other determined to restore our unity
it turns one way then the other looking for me like a mother
searching frantically

i am senseless numb except for this part of me i am all anxiety stupor
i want to be found   oh
i want to be found

my heart hurts
it doesn't stop hurting
it won't stop hurting anytime soon

my heart is me not-me separate as twins born to different mothers as
              incomplete

i say   heart
i mean   show me the way

i say   aches
i mean   instruct me

i say   heartaches
i mean   how long?

a walk with my mom

(for leftover alice who told me i had to write this.
"in your right hand are pleasures forevermore" Psalm 16:11b)

i went for a walk with mom yesterday
i got onto the canal path could not stop obsessing about fucking
        bosses fucking with me
i was so frustrated not to be able to silence my anger disappointment
        fever pain i finally called out to mom just started talking
        aloud to her telling her how lost i was again
when i paused thinking i had just momentarily run out of things to
        say i became aware
               i knew a responding presence
               i was not talking out loud to myself at all
               i was in a conversation

she was no corporeal no holographic being
we were together in some alternative space having slid from parallel
        universes into a crosslands the way two lightbeams can
        overlap mingle particlewaves make waveparticles
        indistinguishably one without losing their otherness
        identities
i did not "hear" her voice as much as i felt it
this is the way a stone-deaf percussionist improvises with a jazz
        band
it's all about vibrations vibrating other vibrations inter-vibrating
        intra-vibrations within
               amongst helixes of interwoven helixes twisting
        vibrant strands tangled spun from a single wound one
        ferocious excruciating slash from which the universe

spewed   our little sun a trembling weeping scar-sign on
         the black skin of primordial   oneness dancing with joy
it was like that except   it was just me and my mom
                                           i was walking along the canal
                                           she was with me
                                           we were having a conversation
                                           i used words
                                           she used something else
                                           for which i have no name

if someone saw me they would have seen an old man walking a
         strong pace uneven gait talking out loud to himself
         sometimes sobbing
someone who saw me might have thought i was not taking my
         medication or in early-onset dementia or maybe just using
         a cellphone they couldn't see from that far away

but no one was on the canal path   except me and my mom

don't think i was out of my body
i was as fully in my body as i was once in hers
more fully in my body than i've ever been
this was not like a dream not like a hallucination
it was certainly nothing like pharmaceutical fantasies chemical
         imbalances
i've had plenty of those i can testify with confidence from my own
         experience :
         my mom and i went for a walk yesterday her death
         notwithstanding we walked
         awhile together
i don't know how or why

i don't believe in ghosts or spirits i don't even believe in life-after-death
this was not like cheap-grace tv hollywood pop-culture tear-jerker fare
i'm not religious
we walked together most of three miles talking :

> me using words
> my voice
> she using her
> new ways of
> engaging with me

when she left we said our usual goodbyes :

> i love you i miss you
> see you again soon

then my body was wrapped by hers she held me as completely
> tightly as tenderly as she   had
when i was born
she called me son
she let me know she would come again she could do that now
i felt her leave me the way sunshine fades from my body when
> clouds come between the light and the place on the canal
> path where i stood with grief-joy dripping on my shoes

as i left the path to re-enter the neighborhood world i saw a mother
> her child each on obviously new grown-up bicycles
> approach the entrance to the path

"swing out in an arc to bump over the curb onto the path stand up
like this" the mother demonstrated explained "if you stay
parallel the bike could slide out from under you and
crash" then waited the child swung out less than her mom
bumped up   over curb onto path   the two rode on
i stood
watched them go out of sight the mother staying just enough ahead
to avoid interfering enough to instruct the child becoming
braver   i smiled   thought
"mom is always helping somebody"   walked home :
i treasure this walk
we shared
and ponder it
in my heart

elegy for sarahjoynelson

she made a list of people to contact   i was on it
five years ago she was my student
a vivacious blonde compact pugnacious as a bulldog
intense focused as a martial artist then suddenly giddy as a
               cheerleader
she led with her wellness packed her illness away
until its weight took her down took her out
she always came back   until now

i remember being surprised even after i'd known her awhile
how short she was how tiny her hands
she was not a small person she was usually
a force to be reckoned with
a beauty who turned heads

when she burned the nick cave cd's for me
she shared her secret
we talked
i don't usually reveal
my own secret outside my family
but i thought it might help her to know—
now i wonder—
did the fear of my decades of pain. . .
it must have been some comfort to her
my name was on her list

we wrote poems we read them
we made up stories told brilliant lies
all of us in each class with her listened
usually because she was fascinating
sometimes because she had a way of demanding it

my mother recently died
when i was 23 experienced my first "breakdown" i learned of her
        depression
she told me of one particularly dark time——i'd never known. . .
i miss her more because of the struggle we shared
tho i never confessed the number of times
i consoled myself with certain fantasies never asked about hers
we just nodded knowing embraced knowing

she prayed to her god
i railed against him

she sang hymns to her god
i wrote poems to fill the void without him

she practiced positive thinking
i turned rage   self-loathing into classroom lectures humorous
        monologs

she always put on a smile   i became an actor
beneath our differences
one common lasting pain one lingering burden : depression

i don't know how my young friend's life ended
nor the immediate circumstances
which made her believe it was time
but i completely understand
what might have convinced her
she couldn't go on

my mom made it to 80
i've gotten past 60
sarah was barely 30

depression is a heavy weight
no matter how long you carry it
i know
some decide
sooner than others
to throw it off
find peace

i'm glad I made her contact list
i'm glad her mother e-mailed me
i'm grateful to have known her a little while

aftergarden

> *("in your body is the garden of flowers" Kabir translated by*
> *Tagore)*

we matter to each other   it i i it   thou-less potted gift lifeless vines
papery blossoms

we care for each other dry rock burning invisibly up in the daylight
atmosphere my sudden heartache the last little chinese girl
unadopted the bottomless abandoned strip-mine

when i began making bread from crushed river-rock eating fossil-
meat from beds where life has not spawned in post-historic testing
grounds i gave up the usual love in popular piano ballads

i've collected over a thousand hammers

my ribs will only expand enough to contain so many ultrasound
supersonic sunbursts at a time all the saxophones have melted

this is it we used to say about true love at first sight when cereal
boxes stood up straight in coffins hung sideways in church
basements modern-kitchens when birds were not
purchased in little crucifixion scenes when picnics didn't always end
up with dry bones iraqi dust-storms

we make only throaty "k" sounds   kk   k-k-k-k-
            kkkkkkkkkkk
            like machine parts grinding themselves passively
            persistently without inspiration
toward ashes

25

i know you're wondering about all those computer chips mother-
boards flat screen plasma monitors bled to death you say yes that's
my argument i have to weep at your extreme fundamentalism

when jesus rubbed two sticks together under the bodhi tree
muhammed kissed the kaaba mirabai headed for siberia to hook up
with emigrating innuit making plans for macho picchu when
chicago's gang wars got out of hand hip-hop went mainstream

i have a good relationship with lumber

nails too have helped me hold it together when the last wine bottles
collapsed into shifting sands leaving little red stains on genesis like
rorschachs after a firing squad luncheon

we make mini-dunes in sandboxes to teach water how to behave

i've had visions of it it has had visions of me   otherwise the sky is
lifeless blueblack   blueblack   blueblack without a story just shrapnel
slashing a cosmos to death

after rare rainstorms certain leaves roots brew for a while in molten
solarity awaken us we
meet there beside the ring of stones beside the long narrow memory
of fluids under a
rotten tarpaulin

we nod knowingly an old married couple one of whom is about to
die the other agreeing it's ok hold on to each other let go

if i'm not the last one on earth   it is   if it's not the final dynamic
force on this hot blue dervish rock i could be nominated

we're not one

we're not always going to be together

we just share this special understanding

i'm only one lotus petal in half a broken fountain beside a mountain
of rubble its concavity holds me until the final word will separate us
from the wet mirror

ah   suddenly   a vowel

dad's first cruise without mom

("i sit here and make no sign/like an infant that doesn't smile"
#20 Laotzu's Taoteching translated by Red Pine)

i am re-learning to be visible like i could always be when i was a boy
hunting buffaloes bad guys in the vacant lots of suburbs where my
father moved us

my father and i always fought different wars held different principles
about fighting wars until we became old men mourning together

i was more guerilla-style he all d-day h-bombs though we both
favored hitler's lil bug for a quarter century of cold war neither of us
had much time for shakespeare john wayne

when mom fell the last time ash clouds were wreaking havoc on air
travel in europe i was stuck in iona abbey 'til after she died my dad
wasn't sure about calling me home we made up for a lifetime of
avoiding eye contact never sharing big manly hugs when we
saw mom's body on the gurney that would roll her up to the
crematorium mouth

i'll never forget dad storming out of the house when i was 10 coming
back awhile later in tears it took 50 years to forgive him for not
saving mom then from weeks of shock
therapy years of valium the wrath of her father's god

now he's off to alaska all alone for the first time in 62 years except
the weeks of fighter squadron alert in the 1950's a year on the
ground in viet nam a week here week there
when mom would visit her sister in another state

i am worrying about him the way i worried about my daughters' first
days of kindergarten
            helplessly   hopefully   grievously   joyously
            entirely out of my hands

i will go to work come home again   i will have supper with his
daughter-in-law my wife

we will talk about how windy it was today how close we have come
to autumn how much work we have to do tomorrow how tired we
always are in the evening will go to bed listen all night for the other
to murmur to move

i will dream again of places i should know people i should recognize
but do not

i will wake myself up wake myself up wonder how dad is doing
alone in alaska   get up   make myself some hot herbal tea
read a couple of poems   go back to bed

i hope dad makes a friend doesn't miss mom as much as i imagine he
will sleep peacefully most nights   i wish i could help him make
small talk at dinner

i'm still glad we can't stop grieving every day
we hold her in common   why didn't we before

the wars are over now it's safe to weep   over so much time lost   so
many casualties

29

dad called from anchorage

dad called from anchorage
he's well
mom is dead
he can live with that
it sounds cold to say it so simply

the tides in anchorage bay vary as much as 37 feet with profound
implications for ships their displacement ratios

dad said he's in shirtsleeves
it was still light last night at 11 mid-september
he slept late this morning went for a walk in the soon-frigid city

the cruise ship turns southward tomorrow

he's enjoying himself he said
he's glad he went
it's just that sometimes he wants to tell mom so many things
he can't
she's gone as gone can be
then he has a rough time for a little while
the next moment keeps arriving before he is completely
                overwhelmed
this is what life goes on means

dad has already learned to ride the space between this one
            excruciating moment its passing
he's like a patient man in a little boat without oars
keeps floating closer closer to shore
he can wait

mom's gone four months now
he has not yet passed away himself
so he can live with that

he's taken a two-week cruise alone
a cruise he and mom did together ten times
everything looks exactly the same completely different
dad feels like an alien a boy a ghost
dad does not know himself at all
but he's getting acquainted

he is not lost
don't mistake his lack of identity for its loss
he's discovering how to sleep   alone
how to watch glaciers collapse   alone
how to eat meals among strangers   alone
how to love beauty without sharing it
how to compose himself over and over again each day he is
            shipboard   alone

i'm ok he said

he didn't want to talk too long

he wasn't going to cry this time

he had to get back to the journey he's on   without me

                                                                              without my brother

                                                                              without my sister

without mom

lament for the apple tree in my high plains urban yard

does the apple tree sigh a little each time a piece of fruit falls
does she long to stand upright unweighted reaching only for the sun
does the tree sometimes cry out in pain for the relentless strain the
                unmitigated heaviness

the tree is divided against itself
the spinning earth forces it to bend bow down
if a season is especially bountiful the tree could split bleed from long
                deep gashes where
limbs tore away hanging like medieval criminals or on the ground
                the way a
soundless suicide lies on the sidewalk after jumping

still her leaves turn upward open like the hands of good muslims
her trunk core branches keep reaching for the light

is she patiently waiting for the late frost to free her
is she moaning
does she sometimes scream with urgency
does she wish she could run away just die
does she feel taunted by the wind's slick promises then betrayed
                after he has caressed her all
day all night disappeared

does she ache for the brittle deliverance of winter dread the slow
        inevitability of spring
does the apple tree resent her perpetual symbolic identity hunger to
        go back to the goddam
garden burn the forsaken place down
does she tire of standing for truth light crucifixion just want to be a
        tree reaching down in this
particularly unsuitable soil reaches up touch the hem of god's blue
        garment

does she bless squirrels birds who nibble on fruits toss them to the
        ground
does she will certain ones to break loose fall with a thud
does the separating stem hurt like a torn hangnail or a scab picked
        too early
does she feel grief like a mother whose babies must leave home
        before they are ready
or does she feel only relief the promise of more relief if only she can
        endure

no one ever eats these apples
does she feel useless
does she believe her suffering comes season after season to naught
does she pray to a vengeful god to become firewood in a
        neighborhood conflagration
        firefighters cannot contain
does she pray to a merciful god to strike her once and for all with
        redemptive lightning

today unseasonably dry hot she is so heavy with ripening i swear i
        hear her begging me
to borrow a chainsaw take this gnarly overburdened life all the way
        down
she is too old to stand like a prisoner in the yard draped with
        bulbous weights teased by the
lying sensuous breeze

does she remember being taken from her native land being planted
        in this wasteland where
only prickly pear bore fruit for millennia
does she remember the giddy wild confidence of youth a lifetime
        ago or have too many
autumns stiffened her memory

i can't look at her any more today
i must turn walk away
later i will bring a bucket collect the fallen fruit
dump it in the trash can for the garbage truck to haul away

some nights when i cannot sleep i hear one two three apples bump
        on the roof overhead
i hear weeping
poor thing

2   little autumn poems

1.   *facebook poem for autumn*

one puffed up plastic bag flaps laughs full of wind
the sun flies broken-winged back to its hole
even the crows have gone underground like beetles
autumn echoes spill over dead bulldozers
wounded shadows writhe in the leaf-drifts
my solitary heart seals its chambers

2.   *autumn poem for alice*

when i close and lock my heart
because the wind is too cold--
i want you to be inside with me
so we can keep each other warm
through the long dark seasons outside

after psalm 51 (a.m.)

too long without words this silence
sunlight washed table-top tea-steam
relentless nothings day after day
mask of uncried sorrow unreleased tears
if i were a lead player   alas i plod

i can't sit still longer than broken leaves in winter wind
breath hardens like ice clogs in the chest
coughs cloud the empty underbelly where
shadows light wash each other dissolve love's pain

i have to go to work
broken glass everywhere on sidewalks driveways avenues parking
          lots
bloody footprints down all the hallways in businesses outside
          classrooms

my heart will be a broken geode spilling its prayers

someday i will remember to drink enough water to avoid afternoon
          headaches

o lord your hyssop o lord my lips

2 little high ku-jazz poems

(with apologies to Basho and Coltrane)

1. *(for juanita)*
blue flames in her eyes.
hospital disinfectant fumes.
blake's infinity in the i.v. drip.
his eternity in the inevitable
plastic cup of warmed ice-water.
her boney hand in mine.
these empty words.

2.
candle.
such a small flame.
such a long cold night.
i am here in my sorrow's cave.
hot bitter tea.
these little word-fires :
my hermit-voice.

iona anniversary

iona dawn-mist on my heart's window.
droplets slide skid across the old panes.
nearly a year ago.
the ancient walls still cold as tombstones.
two names on spring's wintry wind.
someone's respiration.

About the Poet

Wayne is retired from community college teaching, aka "third world missionary work" (the working title of his teaching memoir). He continues to teach teachers working on their master's degrees in education at University of Colorado Denver.

As an artist, Wayne began performing his original poems in the summer of 2000. His performances are legendary for their dynamic energy. He is well known as "magmapoet," and often performs with improvising musicians.

His first chapbook, *Magmamystic*, was published in 2011 by Mighty Rogue Press, *www.mightyrogue.com*.

Wayne was diagnosed with Parkinson's disease in 2005, but keeps an active schedule writing, teaching, performing and facilitating workshops on grieving and growing, healing the wounded teacher, living creatively with chronic disease/pain, and writing as spiritual practice, *www.magmamystic.com*.

Wayne is also a board member and "artivist" with *Art as Action*, *www.artasaction.org*, and a dancer in their "Re-Connect with Your Body: Dance for P.D." program.

www.ingramcontent.com/pod-product-compliance
Lightning Source LLC
Chambersburg PA
CBHW021916040426
42447CB00007B/881